Original title:

Embracing Me

Author: Kaido Väinamäe

ISBN HARDBACK: 978-9916-89-784-3

ISBN PAPERBACK: 978-9916-89-785-0

ISBN EBOOK: 978-9916-89-786-7

Baptized in Authenticity

In the stillness, truth unfolds,
Hearts awaken, spirits bold.
Cleansed by light, no masks to wear,
In the waters, find the care.

Reflections dance, the soul set free,
Beneath the surface, we can see.
A sacred vow, we make anew,
In authenticity, pure and true.

Pilgrimage of the Heart

With each step, a whisper heard,
The heart's path, love's gentle word.
Through valleys deep, on mountains high,
A journey formed beneath the sky.

Light our way, through shadow and doubt,
In every lesson, grace pours out.
Together we walk, hand in hand,
In faith's embrace, our spirits stand.

Wings of the Spirit

Soar above the earthly plight,
With wings of faith, embrace the light.
In tranquil skies, our souls shall glide,
Through challenges, we will abide.

Lifted high, we find our song,
In unity, we all belong.
A melody that calls us near,
The spirit's dance, forever clear.

A Covenant with Self

In quiet moments, promises made,
A bond with self, in truth conveyed.
No more shadows, only grace,
Embracing flaws, a sacred space.

With open hearts, we take the vow,
To honor now, to cherish how.
In every breath, our spirits lift,
This covenant, our greatest gift.

In the Garden of My Soul

In the quiet shade, I roam,
Where whispers of love call me home.
Each flower blooms with grace divine,
In this sacred space, Your light does shine.

The gentle breeze carries my plea,
Amongst the trees, my spirit feels free.
Roots deep in faith, branches reach wide,
In the garden of love, I abide.

With morning dew, my heart drinks in,
The golden rays, the balm for my sins.
Petals of prayer unfold in the sun,
A promise of peace, my journey begun.

In twilight stillness, I sow my dreams,
With moonlit paths and silver streams.
The stars above guide my way,
In the garden where night blooms day.

As seasons change, I learn to grow,
In love and light, my soul's true glow.
With every step, I seek Your face,
In the garden of my sacred space.

The Sacred Reflection

In the mirror's gaze, I find my truth,
A sacred moment, recalling my youth.
Each flaw and grace, a story unfolds,
In the depth of silence, Your love retolds.

With stillness, I breathe in the light,
A reflection of hope, dispelling the night.
What once felt lost now shines like gold,
In the whispers of faith, I become bold.

Amidst the chaos, I seek Your hand,
Guided by visions, a divine command.
Silent affirmations flow from my heart,
In this sacred place, we shall not part.

Through every tear, a lesson learned,
With every turn, my spirit returned.
I see the beauty in each scar,
In the sacred reflection, I know who You are.

In faith's embrace, my spirit dances,
Each breath I take, a life of chances.
The mirror reflects what I've come to be,
A vessel of love, forever set free.

Inner Pilgrimage of the Heart

On this inner path, I tread with care,
A journey of faith, a sacred dare.
With each step taken, I shed my fears,
In the pilgrimage of love, I dry my tears.

Mountains rise high, valleys run deep,
With every heartbeat, Your promise I keep.
Waves of grace in the ocean of time,
In the footsteps of wisdom, I begin to climb.

The whispers of stillness guide my way,
In search of solace, I choose to stay.
A compass of hope, a lantern of light,
Illuminating the shadows, dispelling the night.

Through valleys of doubt, I find my thread,
A tapestry woven where angels tread.
With a spirit unbroken, I journey afar,
In the inner pilgrimage, I'm never ajar.

As the sun sets low, I breathe in peace,
In my heart's sanctuary, troubles cease.
Each moment a prayer, each mile a start,
In the sacred voyage of the heart.

Whispering Prayers to Myself

In the stillness, whispers arise,
Prayers of hope that touch the skies.
For every worry, a solemn vow,
In gentle reflection, I learn the how.

Each morning light brings fresh desire,
To fan the flames of my inner fire.
With words of kindness, I speak to me,
In this sacred moment, I am free.

Images of love dance in my mind,
An echo of faith, a bond that binds.
Whispered prayers wrapping me tight,
In the arms of the day, I find my light.

Among the shadows, I hear Your call,
In the quiet corners, I stand tall.
With hands open wide, I embrace this grace,
In the sacred whispers, I find my place.

As night descends and dreams take flight,
I cradle my spirit, holding it tight.
With whispered prayers that softly blend,
In the journey of love, You are my friend.

Unveiling the Hidden Light

In shadows deep, the truth does gleam,
A whisper soft, a sacred dream.
Within the heart, a spark ignites,
Unveiling joy, illuminating nights.

With faith as guide, we seek the way,
Where love abounds, and hearts can sway.
Each step we take, a path divine,
In unity, our souls align.

The dawn breaks forth, a promise bright,
Emerging clear from darkest night.
A vision shared, in harmony,
Revealing all that's meant to be.

O radiant glow, forever true,
In every heart, the light shines through.
Embrace the warmth, let doubts depart,
With open arms, we heal the heart.

Together strong, in prayer we stand,
With fervent hope, we join our hand.
Through trials faced, our spirits rise,
In love's embrace, we gain the prize.

The Holy Dance of Identity

In sacred rhythm, souls entwine,
A dance of grace, divine design.
The beat of faith, our hearts proclaim,
In every step, we find our name.

Lifted high on wings of light,
We twirl through spaces, pure and bright.
The tapestry of lives we weave,
In every thread, believe, believe.

In joy we move, let spirits soar,
A song of love, forevermore.
Each twirl reveals, our essence free,
In the embrace of unity.

The shadows fade, the truth does sing,
In every heart, a love that clings.
Embrace, rejoice, the dance won't cease,
In every soul, we find our peace.

Together, blessed, we raise our voice,
In sacred harmony, we rejoice.
For in this dance of light and grace,
We find our true, beloved place.

Cradled in My Own Spirit

In quiet moments, I retreat,
To the sanctuary, my heart beats.
Cradled close, my spirit glows,
In gentle whispers, love bestows.

The world outside may churn and sway,
But in this haven, I shall stay.
Embracing all that's deep within,
The essence pure of where I've been.

Each breath a prayer, a silent vow,
To cherish peace within the now.
With open arms, I greet the morn,
From every loss, a soul reborn.

In solitude, the truth appears,
A treasure deep, beyond our fears.
Cradled here in love's embrace,
I find my strength, my rightful place.

To walk with grace, my spirit loves,
In quiet strength, the heart uncoves.
In gentle light, my path is paved,
In every moment, I am saved.

The Soft Voice of Acceptance

In whispers soft, a truth revealed,
Acceptance grows, our souls are healed.
In brokenness, we find our ground,
A gentle kiss, love's voice profound.

With open hearts, we let it flow,
In every wound, the love will grow.
The grace of being, calm and strong,
In unity, we all belong.

The burdens lift, a light embrace,
In every face, the same kind grace.
With tender hands, we weave the thread,
Of love's acceptance, where we tread.

Through trials faced, our spirits blend,
In heart's wide expanse, we comprehend.
Let judgments fade, and kindness reign,
In soft acceptance, no more pain.

Together held, in sacred sight,
We find our truth, our shared delight.
With open hearts, our voices sing,
In soft acceptance, love takes wing.

My Heart's Sanctuary

In quiet corners, love resides,
A gentle whisper, where hope abides.
Within the stillness, grace unfolds,
A refuge found, where peace beholds.

The echoes of a sacred song,
In every heart, we all belong.
With open arms, the Spirit's flow,
Embraces all, both high and low.

In prayerful thoughts, I seek the dawn,
A guiding light when shadows yawn.
The strength to rise, with faith I stand,
My heart's sanctuary, in God's hand.

The beauty found in every tear,
Transforms the pain, and draws us near.
A tapestry of love and grace,
We gather here, united in space.

This sacred place, my trust restore,
With every breath, I long for more.
In silence deep, my spirit soars,
In my heart's sanctuary, love pours.

The Holy Mystery of Being

In every breath, a spark divine,
A cosmic dance, a thread entwined.
The stars above, a guiding chart,
Reflecting love within the heart.

The sacred pulse of life we feel,
In nature's arms, our spirits heal.
Each moment is a gift bestowed,
The mystery pure, in light we grow.

With humble steps, we seek the truth,
The whispers found in nature's youth.
The glory seen in every face,
Reveals the grace of our shared space.

In every trial, a lesson learned,
In every flame, the heart has burned.
The holy mystery forever shines,
In unity, our spirit aligns.

Let faith be strong, and hope endure,
For in our hearts, the light is pure.
Embrace the truth, and we shall see,
The holy mystery of being, free.

The Sacred Unity of Self

In mirrors bright, reflections meet,
The essence woven, pure and sweet.
Within the soul, a truth reveals,
The sacred unity our heart feels.

With every breath, we intertwine,
In love's embrace, our spirits shine.
The dance of grace, the path we take,
A journey shared, this bond we make.

In silence deep, the self finds peace,
A tranquil heart where worries cease.
In every prayer, we seek the whole,
The light within, a cherished goal.

As petals fall, and seasons change,
The self evolves, yet feels the same.
Eternal love, forever grows,
In sacred unity, our spirit glows.

Let every heartbeat testify,
To sacred dreams that never die.
In every moment, pure and blessed,
The sacred unity of self, expressed.

Illuminated by My Own Light

In darkest hours, a flame ignites,
A beacon strong, that guides my sights.
With every trial, I find the way,
Illuminated by love's ray.

The strength within, a force divine,
In every moment, I shall shine.
With faith, I walk this sacred ground,
In light of love, true peace is found.

The journey long, yet worth the quest,
In solitude, my heart finds rest.
Each step I take, in grace I stroll,
Illuminated by my own soul.

The trials faced, a path to learn,
With every challenge, candles burn.
The love I seek is always near,
In joy and sorrow, crystal clear.

So let my heart, with joy declare,
In every breath, a prayer to share.
Illuminated, I take my flight,
Finding my way, through love's pure light.

Celestial Insights

In the stillness of the night,
Stars whisper tales of old.
Guiding souls in sacred flight,
To the truth that shall unfold.

Wisdom drapes the heavens bright,
Casting shadows on the ground.
In every heart, a spark of light,
Eternal love is always found.

Prayer rises like incense sweet,
Carried on the breath of grace.
In the dance where spirits meet,
Unity, our holy space.

Glimmers of the divine spark,
Illuminating paths we tread.
Through the joy and through the dark,
Hearts entwined, our spirits led.

Seek the quiet within the noise,
Listen to the softest call.
In the silence, find our joys,
In the oneness, we are all.

The Holy Canvas of Being

Upon the canvas of the soul,
Colors blend in sacred hands.
Every stroke, a part, a whole,
Masterpiece that understands.

In each heart, a vibrant hue,
A brush with love that paints the way.
Creation dances, ever new,
In the light of every day.

The whispers of the wind do sing,
Of stories lost and tales untold.
Nature's heart, a sacred ring,
Embracing warmth against the cold.

As we gather in this place,
Fingers touch the holy ground.
Every face, a trace of grace,
In this unity, we are bound.

Life's reflections, deep and bright,
In every shadow, light will gleam.
Together, we shall find our sight,
In the holy, we shall dream.

Singularity in Spirit

In the silence, hearts collide,
Echoes of a bond divine.
In every tear, a love applied,
In every prayer, the sacred sign.

One breath shared in holy night,
Pierces the veil of earthly ties.
Soul to soul, a radiant light,
Transcending all, we rise.

In the depths of quiet grace,
The universe begins to stir.
In our eyes, a timeless trace,
Of every wish and whispered purr.

Harmony in every thought,
Resonates through time and space.
In this moment, truth is sought,
In the spirit's warm embrace.

Thus we gather, spirit free,
In the oneness we shall sing.
Together, we are meant to be,
Just a breath, and love takes wing.

Reflections of the Divine

In the mirror of the heart,
Truth reflects in sacred streams.
Every fragment, a work of art,
Shining bright in whispered dreams.

Life unfolds in gentle waves,
Carried by the hands of grace.
In every struggle, spirit saves,
Finding hope in love's embrace.

Underneath the sky so wide,
Every star, a prayer in flight.
In the silence, we confide,
Seeking peace in darkest night.

Divinity in each kind word,
In every act, a holy spark.
Together, let our voices be heard,
In the light, erase the dark.

Surrender to the flowing grace,
In the journey, let us strive.
Through the chaos, find our place,
In reflections of the divine.

Echoes of Creation

In the silence of the night,
Stars whisper of the light.
Mountains rise with grace divine,
Nature sings, a grand design.

Oceans dance with sacred flow,
Waves proclaim what hearts will know.
Every leaf and jeweled hue,
Speaks of love, both fierce and true.

From the soil to skies above,
All of life reflects His love.
Creation's heart beats strong and clear,
Every moment, He is near.

In the earth and skies so wide,
His spirit is our sure guide.
In each sunrise, hope is born,
In His grace, we're ever worn.

So let us walk in sacred trust,
Embracing beauty, love, and just.
For in His arms, we find our place,
In echoes of creation's grace.

Transcendent Truths

In the stillness of the heart,
Whispers of the soul impart.
Wisdom flows from ancient springs,
Truth that cuts through all false things.

Beyond the veil of time and space,
Lies the light of His embrace.
Seeking not in worldly gain,
But in love, we break the chain.

From shadows cast by earthly fears,
We rise above with holy cheers.
Faith our compass, hope our guide,
In the truth, we will abide.

With every prayer, we reach for more,
Transcendent truths we can explore.
In unity, our spirits soar,
Together, ever, we implore.

Let us mingle our desires,
In the heart, let love inspire.
To share the light, our sacred task,
In transcendent truths, we bask.

Nurtured By Faith

In the garden of our souls,
Faith takes root, it sings and rolls.
Every tear, a precious seed,
In His grace, we find our need.

Moments shared in humble prayer,
Lift us up from earthly care.
With each whisper, love unites,
Guiding us through darkest nights.

Nurtured strong by holy light,
Bound together, spirits bright.
In the journey, heart to heart,
Faith ignites a brand new start.

With every trial, lessons learned,
In the blaze, our spirits burned.
Hope and courage intertwined,
In the love we seek to find.

So let us walk this path of grace,
With open hearts in sacred space.
Nurtured by faith, hand in hand,
Together in this promised land.

Anointed with Purpose

From the depths of silence springs,
Anointing soft, a voice that sings.
Called to rise with hearts aligned,
Anointed souls, our paths defined.

In service, we find our place,
Spreading warmth, revealing grace.
Every action, love we sow,
Anointed hands, a sacred flow.

With trials faced, our spirits mold,
In unity, our hearts are bold.
Together we walk this sacred road,
Anointing each other, lifting the load.

Let purpose guide us through the night,
In shadows cast, we'll find the light.
Anointed, we're called to be,
A beacon bright for all to see.

So rise and shine, with voices clear,
In His love, we hold so dear.
Anointed with purpose, we embrace,
Together, shining in His grace.

The Testament of Acceptance

In the silence, find your peace,
Let your doubts and fears release.
For every tear, a lesson learned,
In acceptance, your heart is turned.

Embrace the path that fate has laid,
With open hands, no need for trade.
Trust the journey, feel the grace,
In every heartbeat, find your place.

The shadows fade as love draws near,
In every moment, hold it dear.
With kindness sown, the world will bloom,
In acceptance lies a fragrant room.

Each day a gift, each hour a chance,
To dance in faith, to thrill, to prance.
With gratitude, let joy inflame,
In acceptance, call the sacred name.

The Universe Within

Deep within, a star shines bright,
A spark of truth, a guiding light.
The cosmos whispers, secrets tell,
In quietude, we know it well.

In every soul, a galaxy spins,
Where hope ignites and love begins.
With every breath, a mystery,
The universe reflects in me.

The moonlight dances on the sea,
A mirror of what's meant to be.
In solitude, the soul can soar,
A universe forevermore.

Embrace the depths, explore the skies,
In inner realms, the spirit flies.
For in the heart, the worlds connect,
In love's embrace, we find the perfect.

The Devotion of Self-Realization

In stillness lies the sacred key,
To pierce the veil, to truly see.
With every thought, a step we take,
In self-discovery, hearts awake.

Through trials faced, the spirit grows,
A dance of light in shadows throws.
In honest gaze, reflection blooms,
In self-love, the spirit looms.

Each fault embraced, each flaw made whole,
In the depths of night, find your soul.
Let every moment be a prayer,
In self-realization, find your care.

To walk the path, let truth be bold,
In tender whispers, stories told.
With every breath, a vow, a stance,
In devotion, we find our dance.

A Pilgrimage of Love

With every step upon this land,
We carry hope, a guiding hand.
The heart a compass, true and wise,
In love's embrace, no need for disguise.

The road may wind, the journey long,
Yet in each heart, we sing our song.
Through valleys deep and mountains high,
A pilgrimage where spirits fly.

In every stranger, find a friend,
In every story, love transcend.
Together woven, threads so rare,
In the tapestry, we share.

Let kindness be the footprints left,
In every moment, love's bequest.
For on this path, we seek the light,
A pilgrimage of love, so bright.

The Sacred Vessel of Me

In stillness deep, my spirit sings,
A vessel pure, for holy things.
Within this frame, the light does dwell,
A whisper soft, a sacred shell.

Each breath I take, a prayer on high,
As stars above in night sky lie.
My heart a chalice, filled with grace,
To honor love in every space.

The trials faced, a holy rite,
Transforming dark into the light.
With every tear, a lesson learned,
A flicker bright, the candle burned.

In quietude, my soul does find,
The truth of all, the love unlined.
In faith I walk, a path divine,
The sacred vessel, wholly mine.

Revelations of the Heart

In shadows deep, the heart reveals,
A tapestry of pain that heals.
Each beating pulse, a tale unfolds,
In whispered secrets, hope beholds.

Amidst the storms, I seek the calm,
In every chaos, find the balm.
Divine connections spark the flame,
In every heart, a different name.

With every loss, a gain in trust,
In love's embrace, we rise from dust.
Each revelation, a guiding star,
Leading us home, no matter how far.

The truth in silence speaks so loud,
In open hearts, we gather proud.
Together, we the universe play,
In revelations, we find our way.

The Divine Script of Existence

Across the pages of the soul,
The script unfolds, a sacred whole.
In every line, a purpose clear,
In whispered truth, I draw you near.

Within the chapters, joy and strife,
The dance of death, the bloom of life.
Written in stars, our fate aligned,
In cosmic ink, the love defined.

With each new dawn, a verse is born,
In nature's breath, a promise sworn.
The universe sings a melody sweet,
As destiny and freedom meet.

In sacred rhythms, fate intertwines,
The script divine, in hearts it shines.
Together we compose this song,
In harmony, where we belong.

The Inner Temple of Belonging

Within the walls of silence deep,
An inner temple, secrets keep.
In every chamber, echoes play,
A sanctuary, come what may.

With open arms, I seek the light,
In shared embrace, we find our sight.
Together here, our spirits soar,
In unity, we yearn for more.

Each heart a stone, in grace we lay,
Building foundations, come what may.
In sacred trust, we weave the strands,
Of love that flourishes in our hands.

From every wound, a bridge is made,
In shared compassion, fears allayed.
The inner temple, a vibrant space,
Where every soul can find its place.

A Psalm of Self-Love

In quiet reflection, I find my worth,
A sacred whisper, singing of mirth.
Each flaw embraced, a part of the song,
In the heart's deep well, I know I belong.

With every breath, I cherish my soul,
A journey inward, making me whole.
Grace flows through me, a river divine,
In the garden of self, my spirit will shine.

I honor the light that dances within,
A tapestry woven from both loss and win.
In the mirror's gaze, I see the truth clear,
A beloved creation, I hold dear.

Fear dissipates, like shadows at dawn,
In acceptance and love, my fears I have drawn.
Each moment a gift, I embrace with glee,
In the embrace of myself, forever I'll be.

Divine Mosaic of Existence

In the tapestry of life, colors entwine,
Each thread a story, a purpose divine.
The whispers of ages, they guide my way,
In unity's grace, I rejoice and pray.

Mountains of wisdom rise from the earth,
The songs of creation echo with mirth.
Stars paint the night with celestial art,
In this cosmic dance, I play my part.

Sacred the journey, each step I embrace,
A patchwork of moments, a divine embrace.
The light of the spirit, an ever-bright flame,
In the heart of existence, I find my name.

With humble gratitude, I honor the whole,
In the grand design, I discover my role.
Every heartbeat sings, every breath a hymn,
In the divine mosaic, my soul shall brim.

A Sanctuary Within

In silence I dwell, a refuge of peace,
A sanctuary cradling my soul's release.
Amidst the chaos, I breathe and be still,
In the embrace of stillness, I seek His will.

The sacred space, where love is restored,
In humble surrender, I open the door.
Whispers of grace envelope my heart,
In this tranquil haven, I'll never depart.

Here timeless moments meld into one,
The warmth of His light, a soft, gentle sun.
In each gentle sigh, I find my way home,
In this sanctuary, forever I'll roam.

With every heartbeat, I feel Him near,
In the stillness of prayer, I cast aside fear.
In the refuge within, my spirit takes flight,
In love's endless circle, I am wrapped tight.

The Light of Self-Discovery

In the darkness I wandered, lost and alone,
Yet the spark of the spirit, I always had known.
Through valleys of doubt, I searched for the gleam,
Guided by whispers, I followed the dream.

The journey unfolds with each step I take,
In the heart of the struggle, new paths I awake.
The light of truth flickers, a candle in night,
In the depths of my being, I discover my light.

A mirror of wisdom reflects from within,
In the depths of my soul, where love's journey begins.
With courage as armor, I step into day,
In the brightness of dawn, I shall find my way.

Embracing the shadows, I learn to be free,
In the softness of self, I uncover the key.
The light of self-discovery shines ever bright,
In the dance of the spirit, I take joyful flight.

Pathways to the Divine

In quiet whispers, faith does dwell,
Each heart a story, hard to tell.
With open arms we seek the light,
And walk together through the night.

Paths of prayer, where hope is sown,
A journey made, yet never alone.
In every trial, grace we find,
A sacred bond, forever bind.

The stars may fade, the world may fray,
But love will guide us on the way.
Through valleys deep and mountains high,
The soul will soar, it will not die.

With every step, a trust so bold,
In hands unseen, our lives unfold.
The truth will lift us higher still,
In pathways paved by will and will.

So let us dance, rejoice, and sing,
In harmony, our souls will cling.
For on this road, we're meant to find,
The sweetest peace, the purest kind.

Soulful Surrender

In shadows cast by doubt and fear,
We find the grace that brings us near.
To let go, a gentle embrace,
Of all that hides the light of grace.

In silence speaks the heart's refrain,
A melody of joy and pain.
Each tear we shed, a sacred gift,
Our burdens light, our spirits lift.

When life's storms rage, we seek the calm,
In every breath, we find the balm.
As rivers flow to oceans wide,
Our souls surrender, and abide.

Awake, arise, the dawn is near,
In every heartbeat, feel Him here.
We merge as one, lost in His love,
A journey blessed from heaven above.

So let us trust, release control,
And find the peace within our soul.
In soulful surrender, we will see,
The boundless love that sets us free.

The Radiance Within

In every soul, a spark divine,
A flame that burns, a love that shines.
Through darkest nights, it lights the way,
A guiding star, our hearts convey.

With gentle strength, the light will grow,
As seeds of kindness, we shall sow.
Each act of love, a beacon bright,
Illuminating paths of light.

The radiance within us glows,
In times of joy, in times of woes.
Together we shall rise and sing,
The love that only truth can bring.

In quiet moments, feel the grace,
The tender touch, our spirit's space.
For in our hearts, the light is clear,
A sacred bond, forever near.

So let it shine, through all we do,
In every word, in every view.
For in each life, a tale is spun,
The radiance of the Holy One.

Divine Names of Self

In whispers soft, we speak the names,
Of love and light, the sacred flames.
Each title grants us strength anew,
A glimpse of all that's pure and true.

I am the peace that calms the storm,
The gentle hand, the heart so warm.
In every name, a tale is spun,
A journey endless, never done.

The essence flows, in all we are,
A guiding voice, a shining star.
In vibrant colors, life is drawn,
The many names, the endless dawn.

With every breath, we claim our truth,
In youth and age, in joy and ruth.
For we are many, yet we're one,
In divine names, our souls have run.

So let us chant the names we share,
In unity, a sacred prayer.
For in each name, the truth does dwell,
The divine essence within us, tell.

Reverence for My Journey

In silent prayers, I tread my way,
Each step a gift, a chance to sway.
With humble heart, I seek the light,
Guided by faith, I embrace the night.

Through shadows deep, my spirit soars,
With every trial, my soul explores.
In valleys low and mountains high,
I find my strength beneath the sky.

The road may twist, the path may bend,
Yet trust in Him, my steadfast friend.
With open arms, I face each dawn,
A sacred dance, forever drawn.

In moments still, His whisper calls,
A gentle echo, within me falls.
I walk in grace, with joy and peace,
In reverent awe, my heart's release.

So here I stand, my journey true,
A testament of love anew.
With every breath, my spirit sings,
In reverence for the life He brings.

A Pilgrim's Tribute to Self

Upon this path, I seek the real,
To know the heart, to deeply feel.
In honest gaze, I find my face,
A sacred echo, divine embrace.

With every step, I honor me,
A pilgrim's soul, so wild and free.
In trials faced, myself I find,
A light within, forever kind.

The mirror holds my stories past,
In fractured shards, my truth amassed.
With gratitude, I reflect the whole,
A tapestry of body and soul.

Through whispered doubts and voices loud,
I stand in strength, I stand proud.
For every wound, a lesson taught,
In honor's light, my battles fought.

So here I rise, a tribute rare,
To self-discovery, a sacred prayer.
In every heartbeat, every breath,
A pilgrim's journey, beyond death.

The Celestial Singularity

In the cosmos vast, where stars align,
A singular truth, both yours and mine.
The fabric woven of light and grace,
In unity's dance, we find our place.

With every heartbeat, the universe hums,
A sacred rhythm, that softly drums.
In stillness found, we hear the call,
Of love that binds and connects us all.

From dust we rise, to stardust we flow,
In the depths of silence, our spirits grow.
In moments fleeting, eternity stands,
In celestial awe, we join our hands.

Divine reflections in every eye,
In each sunset glow, the sacred sigh.
With every prayer, we touch the divine,
In cosmic embrace, our hearts entwine.

So let us soar, on wings of light,
Embrace the whole, in day and night.
For in this space, we truly see,
The celestial love that sets us free.

Threads of Divinity Woven

In sacred threads, our fates are spun,
A tapestry of life, weaves us as one.
With gentle hands, the weaver sings,
Of love's embrace, of heavenly things.

Through trials faced, our colors blend,
In moments shared, we make amends.
Each thread a story, a sacred tale,
In unity's bond, we shall not fail.

The loom of life, a Divine design,
Crafting the spirit, intertwining the mind.
In laughter bright and sorrow's tear,
The threads connect, we persevere.

In joy and pain, we learn to grow,
In love's warm light, we come to know.
With hearts entwined, we walk the line,
In threads of divinity, we find the divine.

So let us cherish this woven grace,
In every stitch, we find our place.
Through faith and love, we each shall strive,
In threads of the sacred, we come alive.

A Tapestry of Grace

In the quiet folds of prayer,
Hands lifted, hearts bare.
Threads of hope, woven tight,
Guided by His light.

Each stitch tells a story,
Of trials, of glory.
Through valleys, through peaks,
In every whisper, He speaks.

Colors of faith blend bright,
In the fabric of night.
A design made divine,
In love's sacred line.

Embrace the weave of the past,
For in grace, we are cast.
To carry each burden high,
And raise our spirits to the sky.

In unity, we find the thread,
Together, not misled.
A tapestry, forever true,
Each heart, a vibrant hue.

In the Light of My Truth

Awakening from the night,
With dawn, comes the light.
Casting shadows away,
Illuminating the day.

In stillness, I mend,
My heart, a faithful friend.
Whispers of wisdom flow,
In the warmth, I grow.

Each step upon this way,
Guided by love's ray.
In every breath I take,
I find the peace I make.

No fear in being seen,
In the space, I glean.
For truth, a sacred key,
Unlocks the soul's decree.

Shining bright, I take my stand,
With faith, I understand.
In the truth, I am bold,
A story waiting to be told.

The Chorus of Self-Acceptance

In the symphony of grace,
I find my rightful place.
Notes of love, I embrace,
In the silence, I trace.

Each voice, a sacred sound,
In unity, we are bound.
Resonating through the air,
A harmony, pure and rare.

Casting doubt far away,
In acceptance, we sway.
A melody of being,
In every heart, is freeing.

With every fleeting note,
In vulnerability, we float.
Together, we rise and sing,
In joy, our spirits spring.

In the chorus, I belong,
A verse, both brave and strong.
In acceptance, I am whole,
The anthem of my soul.

Surrendering to My Authentic Voice

In the stillness of my heart,
I hear the truth depart.
A whisper, soft yet clear,
Calling me near, so near.

With every doubt released,
I find my voice, increased.
Letting go of the guise,
In authenticity, I rise.

Echoes of my spirit's song,
Guiding where I belong.
In vulnerability, I stand,
With faith, I take my hand.

Each word, a sacred gift,
In surrender, I uplift.
For in speaking my truth loud,
I am woven in the crowd.

Embracing all I am,
No need for a sham.
In the roar of my voice,
I rejoice in the choice.

Sacred Reflections

In quiet woods where shadows blend,
The spirit whispers, hearts ascend.
Each leaf a prayer, each breeze a song,
In sacred silence, we belong.

The rivers flow, a mirrored grace,
Where hope can light the darkest place.
In every stone, a message clear,
Divine embrace, forever near.

Beneath the sky, where stars unite,
We seek the truth, we find the light.
In nature's arms, we pause and see,
The sacred bond of you and me.

With every breath, a promise made,
In faith we stand, unafraid.
Through trials faced and love's sweet art,
We find reflections in the heart.

Together, we journey hand in hand,
In quiet faith, in this vast land.
The sacred whispers guide our way,
In unity, we rise and sway.

The Light Within

In the stillness of the dawn,
A flicker shines, a light is born.
Through shadows deep, it starts to grow,
A gentle warmth, a radiant glow.

When burdens weigh upon the soul,
The light within can make us whole.
With every tear, a spark ignites,
Guiding us through the darkest nights.

In moments when our hearts feel low,
The inner flame begins to show.
A beacon bright, it leads us on,
Through life's vast sea, to a new dawn.

Embrace the glow, let worries cease,
In every heart, find strength and peace.
As stars align, we start to see,
The light within, our destiny.

In unity, our spirits blend,
A tapestry that knows no end.
Together, we shine, forever free,
Reflecting love and harmony.

Whispers of the Soul

In the silence, soft and pure,
The whispers of the soul endure.
In gentle tones, they call our name,
A sacred dance, a holy flame.

Through twilight's veil, we feel the thread,
Of love's embrace, where hope is spread.
In every heartbeat, secrets lie,
In whispers soft, they never die.

Amidst the chaos, hear the call,
The soul is speaking, one and all.
In quiet moments, take the time,
To listen close, to love's sweet rhyme.

Every challenge brings a gift,
In trials faced, our spirits lift.
On wings of faith, we soar and grow,
Through whispers soft, the truth will show.

Embrace the echoes, let them flow,
In every silence, wisdom sows.
The whispers guide, the heart must heed,
In sacred trust, we plant the seed.

Divine Acceptance

In every heart, a journey starts,
To seek the truth and play our parts.
In love's embrace, we find our place,
Divine acceptance, a warm grace.

Through every fear, through every fight,
We learn to trust the guiding light.
In open arms, we find our way,
To live in peace, come what may.

With each step taken on this path,
We learn to dance through joy and wrath.
Acceptance blooms in fragile ground,
In the silence, that's where it's found.

Embracing flaws, we find the whole,
In every wound, we heal the soul.
In every moment, let it be,
Divine acceptance, setting free.

A tapestry of lives we weave,
In love and grace, we all believe.
Each thread a story, every one,
In unity, we are as one.

The Path of Belonging

Through shadowed woods we tread,
In search of hearth and home.
Each whispered prayer, a thread,
Binding hearts to roam.

With open hands we gather,
The love that sets us free.
In fellowship we gather,
Together we will see.

Amid the trials we face,
A light does ever shine.
In unity, we grace,
A tapestry divine.

Each step a sacred trust,
In faith, we intertwine.
With patience, hope, and lust,
The stars begin to align.

So sing the songs of old,
Let joy rise on the wind.
With courage we are bold,
In belonging, we ascend.

Threads of Identity

In the loom of life we weave,
Strands of truth in hand.
Each story we believe,
Shapes the vast expanse of land.

Through the trials and the pain,
We find a deeper way.
With joy in every grain,
We nurture hope each day.

Colorful threads unite,
In the patterns that we draw.
From darkness into light,
In faith, we stand in awe.

With every tear we've shed,
A lesson we embrace.
In love, our fears are fed,
In unity, we trace.

Let the tapestry unfold,
Reveal what lies within.
Threads of love and bold,
Guide us to the kin.

In Heavenly Transparency

In silence, we reflect,
On the realms of the divine.
With faith, we interject,
Seeking sacred signs.

A veil so thinly drawn,
Where whispers touch the soul.
In dawn's bright golden yawn,
We glimpse the hidden whole.

Each moment crystalline,
Illuminates the path.
In grace, we intertwine,
Embracing love's warm wrath.

The heavens gently call,
In clarity we find.
A purpose to install,
In each heart and mind.

So raise our hands in praise,
To the light that is shared.
In transparency, we gaze,
At the love that we've spared.

Awakened Essence

In quietude we rise,
To meet the dawn anew.
With open hearts and eyes,
We glimpse the sacred hue.

With every breath we take,
The essence of our being.
In love, we find the wake,
Of truth beyond all seeing.

As petals in the sun,
We blossom forth in grace.
In union, we have won,
A world we dare embrace.

From essence flows the light,
Transforming all we touch.
In harmony, we write,
The verse of love so much.

Awakened, we ascend,
In unity, we soar.
With every heart we mend,
Together we restore.

Embracing the Divine Within

In silence, whispers of grace,
My spirit dances in sacred space.
A light ignites, warm and bright,
Guiding me through the darkest night.

With every breath, the truth unfolds,
A story of love, eternally told.
I seek the essence, pure and real,
In every heartbeat, I learn to feel.

The world around me, a canvas wide,
Where faith and hope gently collide.
I walk the path, hand in hand,
With the Divine, who understands.

In moments still, my heart aligns,
A sacred bond that intertwines.
The echoes of prayer, softly rise,
In the temple of my soul, it lies.

Awakening dreams, the spirit flows,
In every challenge, courage grows.
Embracing the light, I find my way,
With the Divine, I choose to stay.

The Garden of Inner Grace

In the garden where silence blooms,
Soft petals whispering gentle tunes.
Each leaf a promise, each flower a prayer,
A sanctuary crafted with care.

The soil rich with faith's embrace,
Nurtured roots in sacred space.
Beneath the sun's warm, loving gaze,
A tapestry woven of holy praise.

Each heartbeat echoes in the breeze,
The spirit's song, a heart that sees.
With every breath, new life begins,
In this garden, true joy spins.

Birds of blessing take their flight,
Singing praises, pure delight.
They mirror the hope in every heart,
In this garden, we each take part.

And as the evening shadows fall,
We gather in peace, answering the call.
In the stillness, our souls find rest,
In the garden, we are truly blessed.

Harmonizing Faith and Self

In quiet moments, truth revealed,
A harmony, my heart concealed.
With open arms, I greet the dawn,
Embracing faith, my fears are gone.

The melody of spirit flows,
Through valleys deep, where peace bestows.
Each note a song, calling me near,
To dance with grace, to overcome fear.

Reflections cast upon the stream,
Illuminate the joy I dream.
With every ripple, faith will sing,
A union of heart and soul, taking wing.

In the balance of life's embrace,
I find my strength in sacred space.
Each challenge met with courage bold,
A story of love that has been told.

Harmony blooms where faith is sown,
In every heart, the light has grown.
Together we rise, together we stand,
In the dance of life, hand in hand.

The Celestial Reflection

Beneath the stars, my spirit soars,
In cosmic light, my heart explores.
Each twinkle tells of journeys grand,
A celestial map, divinely planned.

In the stillness of the night's embrace,
I seek the truth in boundless space.
The universe whispers secrets old,
In every heartbeat, love unfolds.

Reflections of grace in every dream,
Where all creation sings and beams.
From the depths of darkness, hope will rise,
A dance of light in endless skies.

I am a spark in the vast design,
A shining thread in the grand divine.
Connected to all, I understand,
In the cosmic dance, we take our stand.

And when I gaze into the night,
I feel the warmth of love's pure light.
In the celestial realm, I find my way,
Reflecting grace, day by day.

Anointing My Path with Purpose

With oil of grace, I tread anew,
Each step imbued with sacred hue.
In whispers soft, my heart attunes,
To guiding light of silvered moons.

Purpose blooms where shadows fade,
In trials faced, His love displayed.
Each choice I make, a prayer sent high,
With every breath, my spirit flies.

In burdens borne, His strength I find,
With every fall, He redefined.
Anointing joy on paths obscure,
My heart rejoices, steadfast, sure.

Courage found in darkest night,
In faith's embrace, I seek the light.
He walks with me through stormy seas,
With divined grace, my soul finds ease.

The purpose vast, yet gently set,
In fervent prayer, no room for regret.
Each moment carved in love divine,
Forged in trust, my spirit shines.

The Crossroads of Courage

At crossroads stand, the choices lay,
With faith as guide, I choose my way.
Each path unfolds with lessons strong,
In silent prayers, I will belong.

The wind of change, it sweeps so bold,
Yet in my heart, His truth I hold.
With courage rooted in my core,
Each step forward, I seek much more.

In whispered doubts, His voice I hear,
A call to rise, dispel my fear.
With open heart, I forge ahead,
Embracing hope where angels tread.

The crossroad's weight, I lift with grace,
For in His love, I find my place.
My choices bathed in holy light,
Guide me through the approaching night.

With every turn, I feel Him near,
In shadows thick, He calms my fear.
The courage found within His word,
Is a gentle song, forever heard.

An Inner Testament of Faith

In silence deep, my spirit speaks,
A testament where love's heart seeks.
With every prayer, a promise made,
In shadows cast, my faith displayed.

Through trials faced, in hope I stand,
Embracing whispers, divine hand.
Each tear, a letter, sent above,
In essence pure, the gift of love.

An inner strength that cannot wane,
With fervent trust, I bear the pain.
In darkest days, His light holds true,
Awakening with each morning dew.

My heart a vessel, filled with grace,
An inner song, a sacred space.
In faith's embrace, I'm wholly free,
A testament of Him in me.

In stillness vast, I find my voice,
With every doubt, I make my choice.
A journey woven in His light,
My soul ignited, taken flight.

The Radiance of Self-Revelation

In moments quiet, I seek to see,
The radiance born, alive in me.
Each revelation, a gift profound,
In every breath, His mercy found.

Illumined glow in shadowed fears,
In seeking truth, my heart adheres.
The beauty placed in every scar,
Reflects the light, I've come so far.

With open arms, I greet my soul,
In grace accepted, I am whole.
The wisdom learned, through trials faced,
In love's embrace, my heart is graced.

The path I walk, a dance with fate,
In self-reveal, I celebrate.
With faith as guide, I rise once more,
Within my heart, the sacred core.

Each shining moment, a precious gem,
Reflects His light, this divine hymn.
In self-acceptance, I find release,
A radiance born, a soul at peace.

Unveiling the Spirit

In the stillness, whispers arise,
Guiding the soul to open skies.
Beneath shadows, light does reveal,
The essence of love, the heart's true seal.

As dawn breaks, the promise unfolds,
In sacred dance, the spirit holds.
Awake, dear heart, embrace the flame,
In every breath, the world proclaims.

With faith as our compass, we wander free,
In the tapestry of life, we see.
Every moment, a chance to grow,
In gratitude's arms, our spirits glow.

In silence, the truth softly calls,
Through valleys deep and mountain walls.
With each step, the journey's grace,
Unveiling the spirit in every place.

Together we seek, hand in hand,
In the boundless love, we stand.
For in the heart's eternal quest,
We find our home, our sacred rest.

The Journey to Self

Through the path of reflection, we roam,
Seeking the light that leads us home.
With every heartbeat, truth unfolds,
The journey to self, a story told.

In shadows deep, the courage grows,
Facing the worries, the heart still knows.
Each tear a river, each smile a star,
Mapping the soul, no matter how far.

The sacred moments, the fleeting grace,
In the mirror of time, we find our place.
Embracing the lessons, we rise anew,
In the arms of wisdom, the heart breaks through.

With every step, a piece retrieved,
In the depths of silence, we are believed.
A sacred calling, a voice within,
The journey to self, where we begin.

Through trials and triumphs, we seek the peace,
In the still, small voice, we find release.
As the seasons change, we grow and bend,
The journey to self, where love transcends.

In the Arms of Grace

In moments hushed, grace draws near,
Comforting whispers, calm our fear.
Wrapped in love, we find the way,
In the arms of grace, we softly sway.

Through storms of doubt and waves of pain,
With each breath, hope breaks the chain.
The gentle touch, a healing balm,
In unity's heart, we find our calm.

In every struggle, strength is born,
From shattered dreams, fresh starts adorn.
With faith as our anchor, we will rise,
In the arms of grace, the spirit flies.

Together we gather, souls entwined,
In the symphony of life, love is defined.
As the world turns, we stand embraced,
Forever held in the arms of grace.

With open hearts, we share the light,
In every shadow, we ignite the bright.
Through kindness shared, our spirits trace,
Eternally held in the arms of grace.

Holy Revelations

In quiet prayer, the heavens shower,
Gifts of wisdom, each precious hour.
Revealed in silence, divinity speaks,
With every heartbeat, the soul seeks.

Through sacred texts and ancient rhymes,
The pulse of truth transcends all times.
In every story, light breaks through,
Holy revelations, old yet new.

The miracles woven in daily strife,
Painting the canvas of humble life.
In acts of kindness, the divine is found,
In every gesture, love does abound.

With eyes wide open, we seek the way,
In each discovery, we choose to stay.
The echoes of faith, forever vast,
Holy revelations, our shadows cast.

With hearts alight, we journey forth,
Embracing each lesson, understanding worth.
In unity's bond, we find the scheme,
Holy revelations, a shared dream.

Divine Whispers of Worth

In stillness, hear the gentle call,
A voice that lifts, that will not fall.
Each heart holds value, pure and bright,
An ember glowing in the night.

From shadows deep, the light does break,
Awakening dreams, for love's own sake.
In sacred space, we dare to see,
The worth bestowed on you and me.

When doubts arise, like clouds above,
Remember the truth, you're meant to love.
Embrace the whispers, soft and clear,
Your spirit shines, have no fear.

With every breath, a gift we share,
In unity, our hearts lay bare.
Together we rise, a chorus true,
Divine worth lives in me and you.

Pathways to Inner Serenity

In tranquil moments, the soul finds peace,
A gentle haven where worries cease.
Each pathway leads to calm and light,
A journey inward, pure and bright.

The whispers of nature, a soft embrace,
Guide us to our sacred space.
With every step, the stillness grows,
The river of grace forever flows.

Let go of burdens, cast them away,
In quietude, let your spirit play.
With open hearts, we find our way,
To inner serenity, come what may.

In meditation's arms, we are free,
To dance with truth, to simply be.
With love as our guide, we'll find the light,
Pathways to peace in the still of night.

The Seraphim of Self-Love

Cherish the spark that lies within,
A flame of glory, where love begins.
Seraphim watch, with wings outspread,
Guiding each thought, and every tread.

Embrace your flaws, they're part of you,
In sacred mirror, mirrors true.
For every shadow hides a gift,
In self-love's arms, your spirit will lift.

With gentle words, speak to your soul,
A heart mender, a joyous role.
In every heartbeat, let kindness flow,
The seraphim's grace, forever glow.

In the realm of love, we soar so high,
Unveiling the beauty in every sigh.
Together we flourish, barren to bloom,
Inspired by seraphim, dispelling gloom.

Communion with My Essence

In silence, I seek the sacred link,
A touch divine, where spirits sync.
In communion sweet, we merge as one,
With every heartbeat, the journey's begun.

Close your eyes, and feel the grace,
In every breath, you find your place.
Reflections dance upon the sea,
Of love, of light, eternally free.

Through trials faced and battles fought,
The essence whispers all it's taught.
In moments still, find wisdom's glow,
The sacred truth, you long to know.

With open arms, the universe calls,
To witness beauty as spirit falls.
In communion deep, our souls align,
A dance of love, forever divine.

Illuminated Awakening

In the dawn's gentle light, we rise,
Awakening souls, a sacred surprise.
Voices of hope call from within,
A journey of grace, let it begin.

Each step we take on this holy ground,
In whispers of wisdom, love is found.
Hearts ignited by the divine spark,
Guided by faith, we light the dark.

Open your eyes to the world anew,
Embrace the truth that calls to you.
In stillness, we find a tranquil sea,
The essence of life, pure harmony.

Let go of fears that bind our way,
Trust in the light, let it display.
In unity, we stand, hand in hand,
In the arms of grace, forever stand.

Awake, arise, let the spirit soar,
In love and light, we are so much more.
Together we walk, hearts intertwined,
In the dance of life, our souls aligned.

Sacred Union with Self

In the depths of silence, find your core,
A sacred union, forevermore.
Whispers of spirit flow through the night,
Embrace your essence, feel the light.

With every breath, a promise we make,
To honor the truth, for our souls' sake.
In the mirror of love, clearly see,
The divine reflection that is you and me.

Through trials and triumphs, we grow strong,
In the symphony of life, we all belong.
Healing the wounds that once held us down,
In the embrace of grace, we wear our crown.

Sacred moments in solitude call,
To listen and learn, to rise and not fall.
In the tapestry of self, brightly weave,
The strength of spirit, in love, believe.

Together with self, we shall explore,
The depths of being, forevermore.
In this union, the heart shall thrive,
Awakening the soul, truly alive.

The Altar of Wholeness

On the altar of wholeness, we lay our trust,
Fragments of love, rising from dust.
Each piece a gift, a story to share,
In the light of acceptance, we lay bare.

Gathered in unity, all are embraced,
The sacredness of life, divinely traced.
Hands held in prayer, voices raised high,
In the warmth of compassion, we soar and fly.

With every heartbeat, a rhythm divine,
Connecting our spirits, your soul and mine.
In the dance of creation, we find our role,
The beauty of life, illuminating the whole.

To heal and transform, together we strive,
In the garden of love, our spirits dive.
Each petal of kindness, a testament true,
In the altar of wholeness, we are renewed.

Let us celebrate this circle we weave,
With grace and gratitude, we believe.
In the heart of the divine, we learn to stand,
Embracing the wholeness, hand in hand.

Revelations in Stillness

In the quiet moments, truth unfolds,
Revelations of spirit, whispers of old.
The stillness deepens, clarity gleams,
In this sacred space, we honor our dreams.

With the breath of nature, we find our way,
Listening to wisdom, come what may.
Each thought a feather, soaring on high,
In the calm of the soul, we learn to fly.

As shadows dance softly, fears take their leave,
In the peace of the heart, we truly believe.
Guided by love, we journey within,
In the sacred silence, we begin to win.

The echoes of presence, profound and bright,
Illuminate pathways, leading to light.
In the stillness, we gather our strength,
Finding the purpose, the divine length.

So pause and reflect, let the world fade,
In the grace of stillness, be unafraid.
For in revelations, the soul will ignite,
In the sanctuary of being, pure and light.

God's Masterpiece Unfolds

In silence He crafted, the world anew,
Each star a whisper, each dawn a view.
Mountains stand tall, seas gently sway,
In His grand design, we find our way.

Colors of nature, a sacred blend,
Each petal and leaf, a message to send.
Life sings in harmony, hearts beat as one,
Under heaven's watch, His work is never done.

From light to shadow, each season flows,
In trials and joy, His presence glows.
We walk through valleys, we climb the hill,
In every breath, His purpose we fulfill.

Time stands still as we gaze and see,
The beauty surrounding, His gift to be.
Together we blossom, His love instilled,
In unity and peace, our dreams are fulfilled.

As night falls gently, stars paint the sky,
In reflection, we ponder, in faith, we rely.
God's masterpiece unfolds, a wondrous sight,
With hearts rejoicing, we bask in His light.

Guided by Inner Light

Through the darkest valleys, a spark resides,
Within our spirits, the truth abides.
When shadows gather and doubts appear,
His inner light shines, calming our fear.

In moments of silence, we hear His call,
A gentle whisper, guiding us all.
With every decision, we seek His grace,
In the warmth of love, we find our place.

The path may twist, the road may bend,
But with faith as our compass, we shall ascend.
In trials we find strength, in love we unite,
Together we journey, guided by light.

Each step we take, His promise we know,
With courage and hope, we face each blow.
No tear is unnoticed, no heart feels alone,
For in His presence, we have found home.

As stars align in the canvas of night,
We walk hand in hand, hearts burning bright.
With every heartbeat, our spirits take flight,
Forever embraced, we're guided by light.

Chosen for the Journey

In the tapestry of life, we find our thread,
Woven with purpose, where angels tread.
Each moment a blessing, each trial a test,
For we are chosen, in love, we are blessed.

With open hearts, we embrace the call,
Through the storms of life, we stand tall.
For every setback, a lesson we learn,
In patience and faith, our spirits will burn.

Walking together, hand in hand,
Together we rise, together we stand.
In every heartbeat, His whispers flow,
Chosen for the journey, together we grow.

From the highest mountain to valleys below,
In His grand design, our intentions we sow.
With courage we face what each day may bring,
In the dance of life, our souls take wing.

So let us rejoice, as we walk this road,
With love and with kindness, together we're bold.
For we are His children, chosen with care,
In this journey of life, forever we share.

The Vine and the Branches

In His garden we flourish, roots deep in grace,
The vine intertwines, our anchored place.
Branches reaching outward, towards the skies,
In nourishing love, true purpose lies.

From storms we are shaped, through sunlight we thrive,
In the warmth of His love, our spirits alive.
Each fruit that we bear tells stories untold,
In unity and kindness, our hearts unfold.

As seasons may change, and shadows may fall,
We stand united, answering His call.
Bound by His love, forever we strive,
In the heart of the vine, we truly arrive.

With hands lifted high, our voices we raise,
In harmony's song, we share our praise.
For we are the branches, His love runs deep,
In His gentle embrace, our faith we keep.

So let the world know, in joy we proclaim,
In the vine's warm embrace, we honor His name.
Together we blossom, forever we stand,
As children of light, united by hand.

The Altar of Self-Love

In silence, I kneel and pray,
A heart open wide, come what may.
With gentle whispers from above,
I find the strength of self-love.

The shadows fade, light fills the air,
In the mirror, I see my care.
Each flaw embraced, a sacred part,
The altar stands within my heart.

I cast away the weight of doubt,
In love's embrace, I dance about.
For I am worthy, pure, and free,
A child of grace, eternally.

With every breath, I claim my faith,
In kindness to myself, I bathe.
For in this journey, I have learned,
Self-love, a flame, forever burned.

At the altar, I gift my fears,
In gratitude, I shed my tears.
With every heartbeat, I renew,
The sacred bond of love so true.

Finding God in My Mirror

I gaze within, a holy sight,
Reflections dance in fading light.
In every line, every scar,
I find my soul, I find my star.

The face I bear, a canvas bright,
Worn with wisdom, touched by light.
Each smile a prayer, each frown a grace,
In this mirror, I find His face.

With hands held high, I seek the spark,
In daily life, in shadows dark.
For God resides in every flaw,
In love's soft whisper, in sacred law.

I learn to cherish, I often sing,
The beauty in the offering.
In every moment of despair,
I recognize the divine care.

So here I stand, in truth's embrace,
Reflecting back the holy grace.
In every breath, I see the plan,
Finding God within this man.

Holy Moments of Acceptance

In whispered prayers, the heart expands,
To cherish life with open hands.
Moments fleeting, yet profound,
Acceptance blooms, grace all around.

With every struggle, I find a gift,
In trials faced, my spirit lifts.
Holy moments pause the race,
To bask in love's enduring grace.

The gentle touch of morning light,
Brings forth hope, dispels the night.
I breathe the peace, surrender is key,
In acceptance, I find harmony.

For every scar and every tear,
A message clear, I hold so dear.
In life's embrace, I feel the flow,
Divine presence in ebb and glow.

Holy moments, soft and sweet,
In acceptance, I find my seat.
With gratitude, I celebrate,
My journey rich, my heart elates.

Echoes of My Spirit

In the stillness, echoes call,
A spirit deep, I feel it all.
Life's symphony, a sacred sound,
In quietude, connection found.

Reflections of the stars above,
Whisper truths, unfold the love.
In every heartbeat, journey flows,
The rhythm dances, spirit grows.

Through valleys low and mountains high,
I trace the paths where angels fly.
With every step, a lesson learned,
In echoes soft, my soul has turned.

With open arms, I greet the night,
In stillness, I embrace the light.
For in the silence, I can hear,
The echoing voice that draws me near.

These echoes call me to become,
A reflection of the holy One.
In every moment, grace ignites,
Echoes of my spirit take flight.

A Sacred Offering of Love

In the stillness of dawn's light,
Hearts open wide in prayer.
Whispers of faith take flight,
In love, we find our share.

Every breath a gentle song,
Crafted in devotion's grace.
Together we shall belong,
In this sacred, hallowed space.

Hands raised to the heavens,
Surrendering all our strife.
In the warmth of blessings given,
Love transcends earthly life.

As we walk this path divine,
Faith blooms upon the ground.
Every step a chance to shine,
In love, our souls are found.

Let the stars our guide become,
Through nights both dark and bright.
In love's embrace, we're never numb,
We find our sacred light.

Illuminating the Shadows

In the depths of silence, we seek,
A light to guide our way.
Through shadows dark and bleak,
Hope rises with the day.

With every prayer we declare,
The light shall pierce the gloom.
In the heart, a fire rare,
Banishing all sense of doom.

As dawn breaks the heavy night,
We revel in truth's embrace.
Illuminating fear and fright,
With love that knows no space.

Together, we stand so bold,
Voices raised to the sky.
In unity, the stories told,
Of strength that will not die.

Let no heart feel alone,
For we are woven tight.
In every seed that's sown,
Blooms a testament of light.

The Oracle Within

Listen closely to the heart,
For wisdom whispers clear.
In quiet moments, we start,
To unveil our deepest fear.

The oracle lies within,
A spark of divine truth.
Through silence, we begin,
To embrace our sacred youth.

Each thought a fleeting breeze,
A compass guiding right.
With every breath, we seize,
The essence of pure light.

Awaken to the sacred call,
Let the journey unfold.
As we rise, we shall not fall,
In the stories told.

In the stillness of the night,
The oracle shines bright.
Trust the voice, it feels so right,
Leading us into the light.

Awakening the Soul's Anthem

In the depths of slumbering dreams,
A melody softly plays.
Awakening souls with beams,
Of hope that lights our ways.

Each note a whisper of grace,
As hearts begin to sing.
We find our rightful place,
In the love that we bring.

As the sun kisses the earth,
The anthem swells within.
In every life, a rebirth,
A dance that shall not end.

With hands joined in unity,
Voices rise to the skies.
In this sacred communion,
The spirit never dies.

Let the song echo far and wide,
A truth for all to see.
In our hearts, love shall abide,
Awakening, we are free.

In Tune with My Spirit's Song

In silence, I hear whispers clear,
A melody of love, always near.
Guiding me gently through night and day,
In every moment, I seek to stay.

With faith as my anchor, I rise,
In harmony with the vast skies.
Each note a blessing, pure and bright,
In the concert of life, I find my light.

As I dance on the edge of grace,
I feel the warmth of a sacred space.
Each breath a prayer, a soft refrain,
In tune with the spirit, free from pain.

The river of joy flows within,
A sacred current, where love begins.
In this symphony, I find my place,
United with all, a sweet embrace.

I sing to the stars, my heart ablaze,
A hymn of gratitude, in endless praise.
Each moment cherished, a timeless song,
In tune with my spirit, I forever belong.

The Blessings of Acceptance

In the stillness of the heart, I find,
Peaceful moments, gently aligned.
Embracing all that life does bring,
In acceptance, my spirit takes wing.

The shadows fall, but I stand tall,
Understanding that grace covers all.
In every challenge, a lesson unfolds,
With arms open wide, my soul beholds.

The power of love in every tear,
A flowing current, drawing me near.
In the dance of life, chaos transforms,
Through acceptance, my spirit warms.

Through valleys deep and mountains high,
Every step is a reason to fly.
In quiet moments, I find my worth,
The blessings of life, in every birth.

Acceptance whispers, 'You are enough,'
In tender moments, when life gets tough.
With each heartbeat, I choose to trust,
In love's embrace, I know I must.

The Sanctuary of Self

Within my heart, a sacred place,
The sanctuary of self, my grace.
Where whispers of truth gently reside,
In solitude, I take great pride.

In the mirror of stillness, I see,
Reflections of all I can be.
With kindness guiding each new day,
I cherish the light that shows me the way.

As petals open to greet the sun,
In this sanctuary, I am one.
With every breath, I create anew,
A life infused with love so true.

The journey within is where I find,
A tapestry woven, divinely intertwined.
Embracing the lessons, both dark and bright,
In the sanctuary of self, I ignite.

With each heartbeat, my spirit sings,
In the calm of my soul, joy always springs.
Here in my essence, I feel the call,
A sanctuary of self, my all.

A Divine Calling of the Heart

In the whispers of dawn, a calling stays,
An echo of love that forever plays.
Through trials and triumphs, my journey unfolds,
A divine calling, in my heart it holds.

As the sun greets the day with golden light,
I embrace the path that feels so right.
With an open heart and a spirit free,
I journey onward, just meant to be.

The universe speaks in a language pure,
Every heartbeat assures me I'm sure.
With dreams ignited and hope aglow,
A divine calling, I long to follow.

In moments of doubt, I hear the song,
A melody reminding me I belong.
With love as my compass and faith as my guide,
I answer the call, with arms open wide.

In the dance of existence, I find my role,
A purpose awakened deep in my soul.
As I walk this path, I embrace the part,
Of a divine calling, a song of the heart.

The Blessing of Inner Peace

In silence, I find grace anew,
A calm that sweeps the morning dew.
With each breath, a moment's bliss,
I embrace the stillness, a sacred kiss.

The world outside may roar and fight,
But here, within, I hold the light.
Each thought, a feather, soft and free,
In the blessing of my inner peace, I see.

Gentle whispers in my soul reside,
Guiding me as a faithful guide.
In each heartbeat, harmony's song,
In this stillness, I know I belong.

With gratitude, I draw the air,
Deep as the ocean, beyond compare.
In moments of strife, I still will stand,
Finding peace, hand in hand.

Resting my spirit, I softly pray,
For blessings to fill my every day.
In the warmth of this tranquil place,
I find the essence of my grace.

Sacred Songs of Self-Unity

In the echo of my heart's refrain,
A melody of love, free from pain.
Each note a step towards the light,
In sacred songs, I take my flight.

From whispers deep, my spirit sings,
Awakening joy in the smallest things.
Together as one, we rise and cheer,
In the unity of love, I hold you near.

The tapestry of life we weave,
In every thread, a bond we conceive.
With every breath, we're intertwined,
In sacred songs, our souls aligned.

Together we dance in the moon's embrace,
In the rhythm of time, we find our place.
Harmony flows like a river's course,
In the sacred chant, we find our source.

As we gather, hearts beating strong,
A choir of love in a world so long.
In each other, reflection divine,
In sacred songs, our spirits shine.

Paving the Path to Wholeness

With every step, I brave the day,
Paving a path where shadows play.
Each challenge faced, a stone to lay,
In the journey of wholeness, I find my way.

The sunlight breaks through clouds of doubt,
A beacon of hope, my soul's about.
In unity with all that is true,
The path to wholeness calls me anew.

With open hands, I share my heart,
Each moment's gift a sacred part.
Together we walk, side by side,
In the flow of love, we will abide.

In the rhythm of life, we dance and sway,
Finding our truth in the light of day.
With every smile, we're building the bond,
Paving the path, of which we're fond.

In stillness and joy, I breathe and be,
With grace, I step into eternity.
The journey unfolds, and so I see,
Paving the way to wholeness, I am free.

The Wisdom of My Heart's Prayer

In the silence of the night I call,
To the wisdom that resides in us all.
With gentle whispers, my spirit speaks,
The truth of my heart is what it seeks.

Each prayer I offer, a seed of love,
Planted with hope, blessed from above.
Through trials faced and moments rare,
I gather the wisdom of my heart's prayer.

In the tapestry of life, I see grace,
In every challenge, a sacred space.
Lessons learned, colors bright,
The wisdom of my heart guides me right.

Connection deepens with each tear shed,
Embracing the journey, where I'm led.
In gratitude, I quietly share,
The beauty found in my heart's prayer.

As dawn approaches, I rise anew,
Carrying love in all I do.
The wisdom unfolds in daily care,
In the rhythm of life, my heart's prayer.

In Praise of My True Nature

In the silence, I hear the call,
A whispering truth, a light for all.
Within my heart, divinity glows,
In every breath, the spirit flows.

Each moment a gift, a sacred chance,
To dance in grace, to join the trance.
Reflections of love in every face,
In every heartbeat, my sacred space.

Echoes of wisdom, ancient and deep,
Awakening dreams from slumber's sleep.
A tapestry woven with threads of care,
In unity found, I rise and dare.

The call of the stars, the song of the sea,
In every creature, the rugged and free.
In nature's embrace, my soul does sing,
In praise of the life that love does bring.

With open arms, I greet the dawn,
The beauty of truth, forever drawn.
In the depths of my being, I find my way,
In praise of my nature, I rise and sway.

The Sacred Pulse of Existence

In the rhythm of time, we find our beat,
Life's sacred journey, forever sweet.
Each heartbeat echoes the grace we seek,
In silence and stillness, our spirits speak.

The pulse of existence, fierce and bold,
In whispers of love, the stories unfold.
Every tear and laughter, a sacred song,
In the dance of existence, we all belong.

From mountains high to valleys low,
The sacred pulse guides where we go.
In the wind's soft breath, in the river's flow,
The essence of life, ever aglow.

A tapestry woven with every thread,
In moments of joy, in sorrow and dread.
We rise together, as stars align,
In the sacred pulse, our hearts entwine.

The universe whispers, in every embrace,
In the sacred pulse, we find our place.
Awake in the light, we feel the thrill,
In the dance of existence, we are fulfilled.

An Invitation to Inner Peace

In the stillness, come rest your mind,
An inner sanctuary, serene and kind.
With every breath, let worries cease,
In the heart's embrace, find your peace.

The world outside may churn and race,
Yet deep within lies a sacred space.
Where chaos fades and silence reigns,
In this refuge, love sustains.

With open hands, release the strife,
In surrender, discover new life.
Each moment a blessing, each heartbeat a treasure,
In the calm of stillness, find pure pleasure.

Awake to the light, let shadows flee,
Invite the warmth of tranquility.
In every thought, in every sigh,
An invitation to simply fly.

Through the portal of grace, let spirit soar,
In every heartbeat, seek to explore.
With love as your guide, let fears decrease,
Answer the call to inner peace.

The Revelation of My Being

In the depths of silence, I come to know,
The revelation deep, like rivers flow.
The layers unfold, the truth revealed,
In the heart's embrace, my spirit healed.

Each thought a beacon, shining bright,
Illuminating shadows, into the light.
In the journey within, I claim my name,
A spark of divinity, forever the same.

The beauty of existence, a wondrous sight,
In every moment, presence ignites.
In the whispers of love, I find my way,
The revelation of being, come what may.

The sacred truth wraps me in grace,
In the depths of my soul, I find my place.
With every heartbeat, I rise and claim,
The revelation of love, the eternal flame.

With open eyes, I embrace the now,
In the dance of existence, I take my bow.
In the symphony of life, let my spirit sing,
In the revelation of being, my heart takes wing.

The Celestial Embrace

In the stillness of the night,
Angels whisper soft and bright.
Stars align in heaven's view,
Guiding hearts forever true.

Hands raised high in fervent prayer,
Souls entwined in sacred care.
The sky unfolds its velvet grace,
As we seek the holy space.

In murmurs of the sacred song,
We find where our spirits belong.
Each heartbeat echoes divine love,
Uniting us with peace above.

With faith, we walk the hallowed path,
Embracing joy, transcending wrath.
In the light of truth's embrace,
We discover our rightful place.

Hemmed in light, our fears disband,
Together in this wondrous land.
In each moment, guidance flows,
In the embrace, a love that grows.

Alighting the Soul's Flame

From the depths of quiet night,
A flicker sparks, a guiding light.
In shadows deep, the spirits gleam,
Awakening the sacred dream.

With every breath, we fan the fire,
A burning hope, a holy desire.
Flames of faith, they dance and soar,
Illuminating our spirit's core.

Embers whisper through the dark,
Igniting souls, a holy spark.
Together, we rise, hand in hand,
Bound by love, a faithful band.

Through trials fierce, we hold the flame,
In unity, we praise His name.
For every heart, a place to glow,
In the warmth of love, we grow.

Let passion rise, the spirit sing,
Embrace the joy that light can bring.
As fire alights the soul's true aim,
We journey forth to stake our claim.

The Shimmer of Inner Light

In silence found, the heart reveals,
A shimmering truth that gently heals.
Within the depths, our visions gleam,
Illuminating the sacred dream.

Each spirit glows, a star in night,
Reflecting love, a beacon bright.
With every thought, let kindness reign,
In this luster, we shed our pain.

Guided by the sacred flame,
We rise above the world's acclaim.
In gentle whispers, truth ignites,
A shining path, the soul's delights.

Through trials faced and shadows cast,
The shimmer beckons, holding fast.
Together forged in love's embrace,
We shine as one, a holy grace.

In every heart, a light does dwell,
A sacred story none can tell.
As we align with love's pure might,
We awaken to our inner light.

The Holy Grail of Identity

In quests of spirit, we embark,
Seeking truth within the dark.
The grail awaits with arms spread wide,
Holding all we've sought inside.

With every step, we tread the path,
Finding solace, overcoming wrath.
In moments still, our spirits soar,
Discovering what we had ignored.

The search for self, a sacred rite,
To know our worth, to claim the light.
In quiet knowing, we transcend,
Embracing love, our truest friend.

Through valleys low and mountains high,
We chase the dreams that never die.
The holy grail, our hearts unite,
As we awaken to the light.

In harmony, our souls entwine,
Reflecting love, divinely aligned.
Through this journey, we shall see,
The holy grail of identity.

The Divine Embrace of Being

In the stillness, I find grace,
Angels whisper, in sacred space.
Light descends, a gentle flood,
Flowing peace, like holy blood.

Each heartbeat, a sacred song,
Eternal love, where I belong.
In the depths, my spirit soars,
Here I dwell, forevermore.

Mountains high and oceans wide,
In creation, I abide.
Stars align, in cosmic dance,
Echoes of a pure romance.

Hands uplifted, heart exposed,
In His presence, I am chosen.
Wisdom flows, a river clear,
In the silence, He is near.

Breath of life, a gift bestowed,
In each moment, love is flowed.
Transcend the veil, and see the light,
In His embrace, darkness takes flight.

Crowned in My Essence

In the still of twilight's glow,
I wear the crown, the truth I know.
Divine whispers, soft and clear,
In my core, I feel Him near.

Each thought a prayer, each act a praise,
I walk in light, my soul ablaze.
Beneath the stars, the universe sings,
Awakening the eternal springs.

A heart that beats with sacred fire,
Jewel of faith, my spirit's lyre.
In every moment, grace unfolds,
My essence treasured, purest gold.

Crowned in love, I rise above,
Guided gently by His dove.
In the storm, I stand so strong,
In His arms, where I belong.

With every breath, I claim my right,
To shine and share this holy light.
In the dance of life, I take my place,
Crowned in love, I seek His face.

Journey to the Inner Temple

Within the heart, a sacred nest,
The journey starts, a quest for rest.
Through the shadows, the soul will roam,
Seeking the light, to find our home.

With every step, the echoes call,
In the silence, I hear it all.
Mysteries of faith unfold,
In each heartbeat, stories told.

A winding path, both tough and sweet,
In humble prayer, I find my feet.
Mountains high and valleys deep,
In His grace, my spirit leaps.

An altar built of love and trust,
In every challenge, rise I must.
Illuminated by divine light,
Guiding me through the dark of night.

The inner temple, a holy space,
Where every tear, a drop of grace.
In the sanctuary of my soul,
I find the truth that makes me whole.

The Hymn of My Existence

Awake my heart, a hymn to sing,
In every breath, the joy you bring.
With gratitude, I raise my voice,
In the divine, my soul rejoice.

Each day unfolds as a gift from grace,
In every moment, I find my place.
Harmony whispers through the air,
A symphony of love, everywhere.

With open hands, I share my light,
In shadows cast, I ignite the night.
The canvas wide, my spirit's colors,
Each stroke a tale of my sisters and brothers.

Cycles of life, an endless flow,
In the dance of dreams, we come to know.
Eternal truths weave through the song,
In unity, together we belong.

So I stand tall, my heart ablaze,
In every heartbeat, a hymn of praise.
For in this life, both vast and free,
The hymn of love lives on in me.

The Sanctuary of Self

In the stillness, my spirit awakes,
A temple of peace, where my heart breaks.
Light floods the shadows, calming my fears,
Whispers of grace through the passage of years.

Within these walls, my truth will soar,
Each prayer a step to the open door.
Divine reflections in every sigh,
In the sanctuary of self, I rise high.

With every breath, I find my song,
Embraced by love, I truly belong.
Echoes of faith flow deep in my soul,
In this sacred space, I am made whole.

Landscapes of silence, sacred and bright,
Guiding my journey, igniting the night.
Every moment a blessing, grace bestowed,
In this sanctuary, my spirit glowed.

Here in the quiet, the world refrains,
I dance in the spirit, free from chains.
With open hands, I receive the light,
In the sanctuary of self, all is right.

A Seraph's Embrace

In the soft glow of dawn's first light,
Wings of a seraph take gentle flight.
Whispers of joy, a heavenly hymn,
In their embrace, all fears grow dim.

Their laughter echoes through the skies,
A chorus of love that never dies.
With each flutter, they weave a bond,
A tapestry rich, a world beyond.

Through trials faced, they offer grace,
Guiding the lost to a sacred place.
With feathered whispers, they bring the peace,
In a seraph's embrace, all troubles cease.

Hearts lifted high, towards the divine,
Under their wings, our spirits entwine.
Gentle reminders of hope and light,
In their warmth, shadows take flight.

In a moment of stillness, we find our way,
Carried by love that will never sway.
Together in faith, we rise and soar,
In a seraph's embrace, forevermore.

The Gift of Being

In the breath of life, a gift unfolds,
Threads of existence, woven and bold.
Each heartbeat a rhythm, a sacred dance,
In the gift of being, we find our chance.

Every moment cherished, a divine spark,
Illuminating paths, guiding the dark.
Through trials and joy, we learn and grow,
In the gift of being, love's rivers flow.

Awake in the present, the essence of soul,
Gathering fragments to make us whole.
Here in the now, in grace we reside,
In the gift of being, the truth won't hide.

With open hearts, we share the light,
Each glance a blessing, a wondrous sight.
Together we walk on this sacred ground,
In the gift of being, life's beauty is found.

So let us rejoice in this fleeting time,
Embracing each day, in rhythms sublime.
In unity, we sing, with voices clear,
In the gift of being, love draws near.

Celestial Harmony

In the symphony of stars, a melody plays,
Whispers of creation in myriad ways.
Celestial bodies dance in the night,
Drawing the heart towards the infinite light.

Each ray a blessing, each note a prayer,
Tales of the cosmos, a story to share.
In the warmth of the sun, in the moon's embrace,
Celestial harmony fills time and space.

Waves of the ocean, a heartbeat divine,
Nature's orchestra, perfectly aligned.
In every rustle of leaves, a song,
In celestial harmony, we all belong.

Combining our voices, we reach for the sky,
In unity's strength, we learn to fly.
Merging our spirits in love's timeless song,
In celestial harmony, we all are strong.

Embrace the wonder, let hearts be light,
Dance in the beauty, illuminate the night.
In joy and connection, let our spirits sway,
In celestial harmony, forever we play.

Milton Keynes UK
Ingram Content Group UK Ltd.
UKHW021835301124
451618UK00007BA/136